How to Teach...
Guided Reading
Like a Boss

Stephen Lockyer

ISBN: 154421068X

Dedication
Thank you to all those teachers (and publishers) who responded with such passion and support for my initial rant about guided reading. Thanks also to Zoe, an inspiring English Leader, and El & Clare, the Year 3 dream team. #malala

Thoughts/comments
Mr.lockyer@gmail.com
@mrlockyer

Contents

Introduction

Thank you for caring enough about guided reading to want to see how it can be improved in your classroom/ year group/ school.

The 2013 National Curriculum does not mention the term guided reading once. It certainly talks about guidance, and reading, but not in the awkward term that it has become in some people's daily timetable. Ask the children to number their favourite subjects and I'd imagine that guided reading would come quite low down in the list.

While I'm not advocating that we cater for favourite subjects, there is something in the delivery that feeds off a teacher's enthusiasm. A passionate art teacher will get art into any subject judiciously, and the children in their care will love it. Although I believe that many teachers love reading, guided reading has become devoid of pleasure for many. Children can't help to recognise that lack of enthusiasm in the delivery.

For years, I dreaded guided reading. I hated planning it, it was organisationally messy and I only really achieved with the children I was directly working with at the time. My frustrations with it grew; here was something on our timetables every day, with the potential power to be really impactful in the children's writing, but the strictures of it were more damaging than beneficial.

In 2015 I began teaching in an urban Primary School, part of an Academy, in west London, where guided reading was very much on the timetable. What was a saving grace was a child-centred leadership who wanted the children to succeed above any desire for cookie-cutter planning. There were expectations certainly, but the approach was "make it work for the children," so I took this to heart started making guided reading my own. This small book is in essence my journey.

Stephen Lockyer
March 2017

Caveat

I haven't invented anything here - nothing is new, just tried and tested to a point that works brilliantly for me.

Given time, I'd like to back this up with actual data details of progress, but for now you'll have to take my word for it, trial it if you are tempted and experience a much easier, calmer guided reading session, where progress seems almost visible.

Part One: The problem

There are a multitude of problems as I see it with guided reading in its current state. Although I'm basing this on my experience and those I read on social media, so not all of these may be true for your school. Please note I am writing from a Primary-based perspective.

What is unusual about many of these problems have evolved into their current awkward state. We are prone to do this in education, and less inclined to stop and consider why something might be broken. I think it's something we need to get more in the habit of doing if we are going to make real progress.

Moving groups

Many guided reading sessions involve the children moving places or moving to their reading seats/groups. In my experience this is wasteful of time and enormously disruptive. I cannot pin down why this occurs, only that it seems to be standard practice. If the children are to work individually, there is no need whatsoever for them to move and sit next to someone else who is also working individually.

Consider the time a transition takes for guided reading. Better still, be honest and time it. I'd estimate it's as much as two minutes from starting announcement to getting into position ready to work. This, over a year equates to six hours a year, just moving into a position for work which could just as simply not happen at all.

Carousel of activities

The standard guided reading session is shared over five days, and with five groups. This that is 25 activities or tasks that the teacher is planning every week. Hyper differentiation. If each takes just one minute to type out, this alone will take almost half an hour of your teaching life a week. Eighteen hours a year. Madness. I've trimmed this down to four tasks, all related and building on one another.

There is another cost to this, which is organisational chaos – at least, that's how it felt for me. It's hard to keep track of a carousel, yet has that beautiful external view of busyness – the children are all moving or working, so the class looks like they are busy and working hard. But are they?

Interruptions

Next time you are in class running a guided reading session, make a tally of every time you are interrupted or asked a question by a child. Also note down any time you have to revert to 'main teacher mode' with pupils someone in the class, if not the class. I'm going to predict it will be a lot. It's the teacher equivalent of patting your head and rubbing your belly. After a while, we become experts at it, but do our children? It is the equivalent of having a conversation with someone whilst monitoring what your toddler is up to, as well as answering questions.

It may be that you have a TA in class while you are carrying out guided reading. Good for you! In my experience, the children will naturally ask you before them, and consequently, you are more likely to be interrupted than they are. You are also more likely to be scanning the room constantly rather than giving your full attention to your group. This is not something to feel guilty about, but rather correct rather simply with one small change.

Text choices

This is either a text unrelated to what they are being taught (part of a scheme) or a text written specifically for guided reading itself. This is something I also have a bit of a problem with, surprisingly. I might by now be coming across as quite an angry and frustrated teacher, but I'm really not! I just want to do things better, and using a reading scheme is not teaching reading more effectively. I feel it's deskilling our children for the writing we *really* are training them to be able to read. Books written for guided reading are almost more dangerous in my opinion – they might exemplify the lesson point more effectively, but that creates a false narrative. Not much writing is filled with fronted adverbials for example. It is easier to study them in isolation than as a batch at once.

Recording

There seems to be a fear in some camps about any form of recording in guided reading, as it goes against the name itself. After all, it isn't guided writing, is it? If we were going to be really clinical, these sessions should really be called *Guided Responding*. That's what we want them to do, isn't it - respond to what they have read, in a way that guides them toward new understanding. My way of guided reading calls for responses every single session (one orally, the rest written). No-one gets left behind.

You have probably got particular frustrations about guided reading that aren't listed here. These were the ones that drove me to write this however.

Keep your personal frustrations in the forefront of your mind as you read the next section, as you might discover they are eliminated as you read.

Part Two: The solution

Here are my solutions to the problems outlined previously.

Moving groups

I don't move the children unless I really have to. This is normally only on Fridays, but even then I avoid it. I notice a diminishing return on reading, responding and recording any time they work as a group. That isn't to say there isn't a benefit in this at times, I just will seek out *any other way first.*

SIDENOTE: I have the same philosophy with cutting and sticking for any task. I always consider first how I could achieve that activity without cutting or sticking anything. If I can find a way to do this, I do that instead. Cutting and sticking often ends up dominating the time in a lesson task, and it really shouldn't. Case in point - I've seen photocopies of simple Venn Diagrams stuck into books (and have been guilty of this myself, even this year). Time to stick in a sheet - two minutes (and this is being generous). Time to draw two intersecting circles - thirty seconds, tops.

The only group that regularly moves is the Key Group. They read with me, and me alone.

Carousel of activities

The carousel is alluring but is also utter madness in terms of class and time management. I'm the first to admit that admit my admin is chaotic, but it does result in me trying hard to develop shortcuts as quickly and as painlessly as possible.

The most unattractive option of the carousel has to be the 'invent 25 stretching 20-minute activities each week' task. I am more than able to do this, but takes such a stretch of time that we tend to cut and paste, changing the number of sentences the children write, and so on.

I start by looking at the learning objective I'm trying to achieve. These are taken directly from the National Curriculum (and at my school, are written as an "I am learning to …" statement), based on two key details – what the children in my class need at that point in time, and then what fits with our current Literacy needs (whether we are studying fiction or non-fiction for example).

I then build four step tasks to get to a strong understanding of this objective. They follow this basic pattern.

- IDENTIFY
- COMPARE
- CONTRAST
- APPLY

Every single child carries out an activity based around four tasks over the week. The fifth task is to read with me, and this is balanced over the week.

The children are split into five groups, with a maximum of six per group. They are banded by actual reading ability, and viscous in nature (at least one child moves each week on average; as I write this, I moved four children last week).

There are two types of group change; the Event, where moving up or down a group is significant (and often gets a response from the parent if it is the 'wrong' group.

The other type of group move is the one I prefer, but takes more organisation; in this one, children more regularly into the group they are best suited to learn from. It happens with such regularity, that I collect my key group by standing next to an open door and listing the children that need to line up in front of me. They are imaginatively named Monday group, Tuesday group and so on.

Sidenote: However you dress this, children suss their groups exceptionally quickly. My daughter, who was six at the time, told me she was in Pentagon group for maths, which was the second highest. "What is the top group called then?" I asked. She looked at me dumbfounded. "Hexagons of course!" We identified the rest. Circles sat on the carpet with the teacher.

I group my children based on reading speed, intonation and understanding, and start the week with the weakest readers, who often need the help to decode the text for the following tasks.

So, the tasks. Here is how they operate:

	Group A	Group B	Group C	Group D	Group E
Monday	KEY	Task 1	Task 1	Task 1	Task 1
Tuesday	Task 1	KEY	Task 2	Task 2	Task 2
Wednesday	Task 2	Task 2	KEY	Task 3	Task 3
Thursday	Task 3	Task 3	Task 3	KEY	Task 4
Friday	Task 4	Task 4	Task 4	Task 4	KEY

As you can see, almost all the most of the time, the class are doing essentially the same task. There is of course differentiation in expectations, and sometimes in texts (more later), but the fact they are on the same task helps in myriad of ways:

The TA, who supervises guided reading, only has to track one or two activities, making their life easier.

They can also model tasks to those who struggle more with reading, as they read at the beginning of the week, so are stepped back one place in the tasks. What this means is that someone only slightly better than them will have already done the task they are on the day before, so this can be talked through and shown to them as a model *and* as a level of expectation. This of course transfers across all groups but the last group.

Interruptions

This is the real revolution in my guided reading. I take one group, leaving my TA to support and hostess the rest of the class. I actually physically take this group out into an intervention area or empty classroom. This has *transformed* my sessions. No interruptions, a new space, a free place to read and talk and respond. It's funny how sometimes even new surroundings are incentive enough, given the right pitch.

You might think this unfair on my TA. We've talked about it extensively, and it really isn't. She is left with 20 children, all working independently on tasks, and can support quite freely. On our return, I find a class happily and quietly beavering away, desperately trying to 'beat the tasks' which essentially means complete the task they are on and jump a day. We try to make this just out of reach. It allows us to be really focussed on presentation, full sentences, and thoughtful work.

Text choices

If something really places a bee in my bonnet, it is dummy texts. If you are at all able to, eliminate them from your lessons.

Instead, use the key text you are studying, or find something relevant online and create an extract. If they are reading it for twenty minutes, it's going to be an extract anyway, so make it fit for purpose. A list of these suggested texts can be found at the back in Appendix A.

My measure is that it should take around five minutes for the top group to read aloud, roughly. This equates to two pages of normal A4 text, or four pages of a paperback. In the past few weeks, I've used:

- An extract from the book;
- An instruction guide on reading your pulse (this had a data table too);
- Four pages from a Horrible history;
- Two pages from the Teachers Notes for a Museum.

They get their extracts on a Monday, and either staple them into their books or file them (bin them) at the end of the week.

I know that this is less than ideal from an environment point of view. The two main reasons I use paper versions rather than the more green iPad versions are:

Over a week, these will often be covered in highlighters, underlining and notes. I know that many Computing teachers will rush forward and say that this is possible on the iPad with any number of Apps, but not to the same extent, I promise you.

I also require the children to follow with their fingers when in the Key Group for almost all the activities. This just can't be recreated using iPads.

I always print 6 more than the children in my class for the Key Group. I have also discovered (by accident) that those children who struggle prefer to use A3 versions of the text (expand A4 on your photocopier by 141% to achieve this). These A3 versions are coveted by all, but take up a lot of desk space.

*SIDENOTE: We use blank oversized exercise books for guided reading. We call these the big yellow books, because they are big and yellow. I completely love them. I wonder how much time Primary teachers spend trimming paper so it fits in books. **And***

sticking sheets in. And throwing away paper. *It's crazy when you stop to think about it. Even sticking it into a blank book seems madness, but it's as close to a compromise as I'm willing to go, as I hate folders. They make me disorganised.*

Recording

In my planning, I map out the four tasks under my Learning Objective. I then cut and paste this into an A4 sheet of paper, with the tasks on one side, and a space for answers on the other.

I print this in colour on Monday morning and the first two children in class stick them in for everyone else. That way, it's almost totally automated. I should really train the children type and print these out for me, but perhaps that's a step too far...

I do expect the children to write in tasks.

Let's take one recent learning objective as an example. Note that each task involves reading, rereading, writing, comparing, thinking and contrasting.

I design them by thinking about what I'd like the child to be able to do by the end of the week - which is invariably to be able to read the extract with confidence and understanding. That's all I want, the tasks just assist that process.

LO: I am learning to use technical words

Task 1 (Identify)	Read the text TWICE and highlight ten words you are unfamiliar with. Underline the words you think are related to this topic.
Task 2 (Compare)	For each of the underlined words, read them in their sentence and write down a definition of what you *think* they mean.
Task 3 (Contrast)	Check your definitions against actual definitions in the dictionary or on iPads. Give two ticks if you were right, one tick for almost right, and write the true definition if you were wrong
Task 4 (Apply)	Write new sentences featuring these words correctly.

SIDENOTE: I mentioned earlier that the children try hard to work to be one task ahead. If that is the case, my TA or I will add an additional depth task for them to complete on either Thursday or Friday.

The verbs beside each task are for me only, and not for the children. I'm not sure if they fit with Bloom's Taxonomy, but I know that they work well as stepped progress, which is fine with me.

As I've taught more and more, and read even more, the main driver of progress seems to be the golden skill of 'comparing and contrasting.' My tasks encourage this from the second task onward, from the second day onward.

I was considering a definition of the purpose of education this morning, and came up with 'enabling children to use existing skills and knowledge to solve new problems' – something I hope my tasks do every week.

Part Three: Designing your tasks

The most complex part of guided reading is designing suitable tasks for the children to complete over the week.

I favour the narrative task approach – something that builds on previous work, so could be completed as a whole if necessary. We in Primary have drifted toward more disparate tasks, where they either learn or practise a skill in isolation. But by creating a narrative arc, these skills become connected and purposeful.

Here are the four task themes again:

Identify
Compare
Contrast
Apply

As stated previously, they progressively build on higher-level skills in a way which challenges them to apply previous knowledge to a new text, yet are never so out of reach that they become unobtainable. I also try wherever possible to have the previous work in view, using the **bansho** method of teaching, so that they can 'step themselves backward' if they find themselves stuck.

Lesson Objectives

Start from the objectives – what are you hoping that the students will achieve by the end of this week. Make this objective but attainable by all.

The best place to find your objectives is to marry the National Curriculum aims with *what your class needs most next* to progress.

The National Curriculum is particularly specific when it lists aims for reading. In Years 3 and 4 this is entitled Comprehension – understanding of the text – so this is should be the driving force for all objectives.

Identify

I actively use highlighters, coloured pencils and underlining at this point. I encourage mutilation of the text.

This task is designed so that the children will look carefully and unpick the text for specific traits of the text itself.

To illustrate this, here are all the reading objectives for Year 3, with a sample Identify task related to each objective. You'll see how each task seeks to have the children identify each objective trait in the chosen text straight away. If the children can't do this, how else are they going to progress?

National Curriculum Objective	IDENTIFY task
listening to and discussing a wide range of fiction, poetry, plays, non-fiction and reference books or textbooks	Write down five questions you'd like answered about the text
reading books that are structured in different ways and reading for a range of purposes	Next to each paragraph, write down the purpose of that paragraph
using dictionaries to	Identify all the

check the meaning of words that they have read	words which you are unsure of in meaning
increasing their familiarity with a wide range of books, including fairy stories, myths and legends, and retelling some of these orally	Summarise each paragraph in six words
identifying themes and conventions in a wide range of books	Write down the themes which emerge
preparing poems and play scripts to read aloud and to perform, showing understanding through intonation, tone, volume and action	Read through the poem and highlight the words you would emphasise if reading aloud
discussing words and phrases that capture the reader's interest and imagination	Underline the words and phrases which capture your imagination
recognising some different forms of poetry [for example, free verse, narrative poetry]	What type of poem is it? Choose words which describe the poem and write them next to the most

	relevant section
checking that the text makes sense to them, discussing their understanding and explaining the meaning of words in context	Underline the parts of the text which don't make sense to you
asking questions to improve their understanding of a text	Highlight the sections which don't make sense
drawing inferences such as inferring characters' feelings, thoughts and motives from their actions, and justifying inferences with evidence	Underline the sections of text which describe a character's feelings in green, and thoughts in red
predicting what might happen from details stated and implied	Write what you think happens next in 6 words, 20 words, then 50 words
identifying main ideas drawn from more than one paragraph and summarising these	What is the main idea from each paragraph? Write these in 6 words
identifying how language, structure, and	List how the language helps

presentation contribute to meaning	you to understand what is being written
retrieve and record information from non-fiction	Underline all the facts in green
participate in discussion about both books that are read to them and those they can read for themselves, taking turns and listening to what others say	Highlight all the sections of the text which help you understand the whole text in green, and the parts you don't understand in blue

As you will have seen, the tasks are wide and mostly open-ended.

I use the 6/20/50 summary model a huge amount, with good reason. Summarising a paragraph into just 6 words is proven to distil an idea down into its key message. Asking children to expand this to 20 words encourages them to flesh this out, and 50 words reinforces this further. Many children in Year 3 can manage to write all three parts in 30 minutes, given practice. I have found that training them in this technique using fairy tales (6 word headline, 20 word text message, 50 word summary) works brilliantly.

Every task after this builds on what they have produced in the Identify task, so if you are going to deep mark one task in the week, this is the one to turn your greatest attention to. While this might sound ambitious, it really doesn't take too long. Bear in mind that if the first task isn't completed correctly, all the other tasks will potentially suffer too. It is worth the effort.

Compare

It seems sometimes that teachers are unsure quite the difference between comparing something and contrasting something. In the guided reading sense, I attribute this as comparing the text to something similar – identifying matching traits if you like.

By doing this, you are enabling the children to seek out the main features and themes of the text; how they are presented, and more importantly, why they are presented in the way that they are.

To ensure that you are focusing on comparisons, try using one of the words below as your leading task verb: *analyse, measure, study, balance, collate, consider, examine, inspect, scan, separate, match up, and match up.* All of these words help to specify the skill you are asking the children to complete.

You don't necessarily have to have a similar text for the children to compare against; in fact, I believe it helps if you don't. By not having a comparable text for some tasks, it enables you to draw from their responses the form and structure of similar texts from memory. If they can only identify two features of a recipe text purely from recall for example, that should be the focus of your next guided reading. The gaps in their knowledge and recall should feed your planning, not the other way around.

Having the children create these comparisons as an adjunct text is an excellent way of removing the pressure of creating a narrative prose, which even at Year 3 is something the children feel inclined to do.

Adjunct texts are any ways in which the children can record their ideas without writing prose (which should by default connect and flow, making it one of the worst ways to record ideas).

The most common way to do this is to use a mind map or spider diagram. In my experience, children need training in how to use this effectively, as well as ways to spur on ideas. Key words and connecting themes can help with this process, as can 'swap and add' opportunities within their groups.

Contrast

This is a much higher order thinking skill, and forces the children to look at the differences between two texts – by doing so, it will highlight features of each.

Try to phrase a contrast task by framing it using firstly a scaffolded model and then gently removing the scaffold to lead thinking to the text itself. The first part of this might be something like this:

Feature	Text	Recipe
Layout		
Writing style (formal/informal)		
Active/passive voice		
Sentence types		
Technical language		
Facts / opinions		
Tense		

Of course, contrasting a mountain to a river is easy – they are so different. Texts are much harder, so require more thought and potentially prompts for the children in order to get them onto the right path for completing the task.

When they are comfortable with using the category features, remove the feature list. Their answers will show you which are recalled most regularly, and thus which ones you need to focus on (i.e. the ones they miss out).

I have found the contrast task the most challenging for children, so ensure your scaffolding is secure and available for all until it is second nature (in my experience, this can take up to two terms if they are unused to interrogating a text in this way).

It may be worth having the feature list available as a strip to stick into books by the children who need them most.

If you are still struggling with this type of task, a simple question can get the children explaining differences in a really quick manner: "why is this text *not* a poem?"

You'll end up with answers such as, "A poem is laid out differently to a recipe, which uses numbers to guide you through what to do." Contrast nailed.

Apply

If we return briefly to my definition of education being to use existing knowledge and skills to solve new problems, this perfectly encapsulates what the Apply task should do.

For technical words, this should be applying these in new sentences.

For facts, it should be applying them in new contexts.

For intonation, this should be to apply the correct intonation when reading the poem aloud.

This doesn't necessarily have to be a large writing task; simply a demonstration of how to use this skill they have studied in a new context is useful.

There are 17 reading strands in Year 3, so you effectively have two chances for the children to take on the skill and demonstrate it – no pressure! In order to complete this successfully, you need to ensure that the children could apply this in a setting other than their guided reading session. It is now more than ever that you should utilise foundation subjects to highlight the opportunities for comparing, contrasting and applying new skills. History and Geography lend themselves well, but try and think more creatively. Using 'odd one out' sets of pictures in Art for example can help to encourage compare and contrast tasks quickly and easily, with no writing from the pupils but huge levels of thinking and thoughtful contributions. Rather than showing them seven pointillist paintings, show them several pointillist paintings juxtaposed against a range of other genres. What is similar? What is different? This is when Venn diagrams really come into their own. Don't just hoard them for Maths.

Part Four: Guided Reading - Key Group Sessions

This is my favourite part, developed over the past year (if I'm honest), and coalesces everything I know about reading for depth into fifteen minutes of pure joyful teaching. Seriously.

They follow the same rough pattern, which my class all know, but I've never written down (until now). I have noticed that I introduce each activity with its name rather than an explanation. The children

SIDENOTE: If anyone can't pronounce a word, they ask their group for help. We have a word for this, which is currently 'Squad,' I'll only say the word correctly if the rest of the group can't. This takes a lot of willpower - we are almost primevally prone to stepping in during reading aloud. If I do say the correct pronunciation, they all repeat it at the same time.

The following pages outline the activities we do in brief.

From the right

Everyone reads one or two sentences from my right, going around. This is my equivalent of a warm up. It also allows me to check they are all at roughly the same reading level really quickly. Children do ebb and flow, and I try to move the children to exactly the right reading group as quickly as possible i.e. the following week. As stated previously, if this is done often enough, it is more of a transition than an event for the children.

Every half term or so, I will hear all the class read the same few passages group after group, just to align my grouping. This is a really useful task, and uses my 'I read in Guided Reading' stamp for their reading diaries. I bough this from Amazon for a few pounds, and if the children behave, they get to stamp it in their books themselves. The easiest motivation EVER.

This is such a common occurrence that the children know exactly what to do, and will often stat reading unprompted.

Mind the gap

We love this game. I read the next part of the extract, and miss out key words. They simply have to say the missing word. They all have to follow with their finger, even the top reading group.

One big problem with guided reading is the speed at which children are switched off if it isn't their turn. This then leads to the inevitable 'where are we?' question WHICH IS THE BANE OF EVERY GUIDED READING SESSION EVER. Hand on heart, this now happens perhaps once or twice a week.

I tend to miss out the words the previous group has made a mistake with, and allow for it to be a small discussion point at times too. Asking the children to break down the word is extremely helpful.

Fill the gap

This is a variation on 'Mind the gap', and is designed to make the children consider synonyms for words within the text.

It is best used on what you might know as Tier Two words – those that aren't common (that, of, who), nor those that are technical and specific to a text (isobar, metatarsal).

It not only encourages children to consider alternatives that fit the context of the text, it allows you to develop quick conversations about the difference in words – staring rather than peeking are synonyms of each other, but have subtle differences (otherwise we'd only need one word). What message does using one word over another make?

Every other

This is used to model reading speed, emphasis, punctuation use and general intonation.

I read the first line, the group read the second line, I read the third, and so on. This might mean I stop mid-sentence; the children have to pick it up so it flows as if we are one voice. This is the one we spend most time reworking together - teaching them the skills outlined above cannot be underestimated. You can *hear* the difference this task alone makes from one session to the next.

It is worth unpicking complex sentences with this task, such how to read a sentence with lots of punctuation or direct speech. I'll have the children reread it if they use monotone voice (which I call Satnav reading).

Echo Reading

This operates on a sentence-by-sentence basis. Child 1 and 2 read the first sentence together (however long or short), Child 2 and 3 read the second sentence together, then 3 and 4, and so on. They support each other in their reading, and can be very tender together when this occurs.

I don't do this activity as much as I should, as they do get quite confused by it at times!

This really encourages the children to read with intonation and also helps them to follow the text carefully. Try to encourage as much flow as is possible. The more canny children will count ahead and work out what sentence they will be reading.

Interrogation

Give the children one paragraph to read alone, twice. They have to look at it really carefully, and encourage them to follow with their fingers even for this part.

Next, ask them as a group a series of quickfire questions. I don't keep a tally physically of who answers what (but probably should), but do make mental notes of who is struggling.

Make this task fun. The children love it. Here are some sample questions:

- Find a word which means large
- Find a word which is the opposite of hungry
- Find a word ending -ing
- Find a word which conveys this is written in past tense
- How many commas are there?
- Find a word with a double lettering
- How many times is a pronoun used?
- What did the cavemen build (text reliant knowledge)
- Find the shortest sentence

I make these up as they are reading the passage, but you could easily write them beforehand if you wanted to prepare further. A set of further ideas can be found in Appendix B.

Some children can have difficulties with specific question. At times like this, give them a further clue, such as "line 4" or "near the beginning." What the children will do is read the text again, more closely, examining each word or phrase more thoroughly. This really is reading for meaning, and can help you ascertain who is reading the words and who understands the text in context.

Jump around

This is probably the most popular activity we do. We read the passage, but as soon as I say your name, you have to start reading. I say names a LOT - sometimes every three words or so. They are all intensely reading, waiting for their turn. I am fairly sure I stole this idea from Doug Lemov - please let me know if this is true. Jumping around keeps everyone on his or her toes. Me included!

At times, I will give one child just a few words to say before jumping to another child. This often has the effect of making them more desperate to read aloud, so use it for your reticent reader in the group.

Sales Pitch

This is our last activity. One person has to try and sell the writing to the rest of the group, and another one has to tear it apart. What they are actually doing is critiquing the writing style and content. I really push them to give me definitive answers and statements rather than "it's really interesting," as that says nothing.

To counter this, encourage the use of comparative verbs in their answers, my golden word being 'because.' Perhaps one of my most used resources are a set of laminated cards saying 'because' on them, which they earn every time they use it correctly. I'm perfectly happy to accept I have gamed its use, but don't care as it works so effectively, and models use/misuse so effectively.

Appendix A: Real Life Texts

Below is a list of texts, which you can use for guided reading and which are also relevant for the children.

Blog post
Game instructions
Newspaper article
News from the Internet
Pages from a fiction book
Pages from a non-fiction book
Recipes
Reviews on Amazon (great also for Grammar Detective lessons!)
Advertisements
Cereal packets
Instructions for a new electronic device.

SIDENOTE: I once riffed with my eldest son on how irrelevant some of the writing tasks were in Primary. "The reason we write diary entries for something historical is that no-one writes a diary any more; they write blogs." Too true, Henry. Writing can be inauthentic at the best of times in school; it's far better to write something that they are actually likely to write than to shoehorn a writing genre in which fits the objective rather than the writing environment the children write within.

Appendix B: Questions for Interrogation Tasks

If you are stuck for questions to ask during the interrogation task, here are some you could use.

You might find it helpful to choose the passage you want to interrogate in advance (it should be around 6-8 lines ideally), then highlight the words you want them to seek out, underline key phrases and circle key facts.

Find me:
- A word ending in –ing
- A word ending in –ed
- A word with two letters together
- A name
- A fact
- A subordinate clause
- A fronted adverbial

How many:
- Commas are used

- Full stops are there
- Sentences are there
- Characters are mentioned

Think of:
- A word in the text which means x
- A word which means the opposite of x
- What e author meant by the phrase x

General:
Who is speaking?
What tense is being used?
When did this happen
What clues tell you about the setting?
What happens next?
What word might be used in a retelling?
What word wouldn't you find in this text?
Who is this written for?

Remember to make the questions fast and quickfire.

Appendix C: Guided Reading Tasks

- From the right
- Mind the gap
- Fill the gap
- Every other
- Echo reading
- Interrogation
- Jump around
- Sales pitch

I've found that the optimum time for a guided reading session is around 20 minutes. Done correctly, it will be the most productive and satisfying twenty minutes of your teaching day.

Appendix D: Unfamiliar words in context

One book I discovered after writing about guided reading was "Bringing Words to Life" by Isobel Beck et.al (Guildford Press, New York, 2002). I would urge you to buy and consume this book!

It has completely changed my viewpoint about words in context being the best way to develop vocabulary. Put simply, words need to be taught, refined and developed over time, and below is the strategy I now use for unfamiliar words in a text.

Route in for an unfamiliar word:
- Contextualise the word within the story;
- Ask the children to repeat the word correctly;
- Explain the word in child-friendly language;
- Provide examples in context outside of the story provided;

- Ask the children to interact with the word in a context they are familiar with;
- Repeat the word once more.

I have used this in guided reading lessons, normal literacy lessons and most especially in one-to-one reading sessions with the children, when they come across an unfamiliar word. For simpler texts, the authors suggest introducing a word which could help to explain some of the concepts in the story.

Final thoughts

As may have come across, I am itchy to improve and improve the practice of fellow teachers and myself. I want to reduce unnecessary workloads, pointless tasks and hollow learning admin. I hope that you have found this book useful in renewed thinking about guided reading. If you can think of another theme I should write for the "**_Like a Boss_**" series, please do email me using **mr.lockyer@gmail.com**, or message me on Twitter using **@mrlockyer**.

I have written two books on ideas and planning for the publisher Bloomsbury, and links to buy them and extra resources can be found here:
http://www.bloomsbury.com/author/stephen-lockyer

This is my rather clumsy Amazon Author page, should you be interested:
https://www.amazon.co.uk/Stephen-Lockyer/e/B00MS7DNYS

Ending

Thanks for reading this! If you feel I've missed something out, or would like me to expand on a part, let me know.

I wrote this because changing guided reading, and having a leadership which allows me to tinker and refine something, has made an enormous difference to both my keenness for guided reading, and the reading of the children themselves.

Printed in Great Britain
by Amazon